· SUPER FACTS ·

AIRCRAFT

ANDREW KERSHAW
AND MARILYN GAYLE

DERRYDALE BOOKS
New York

Contents

Copyright © Grisewood & Dempsey Ltd. 1980, 1985

This 1992 edition published by Derrydale Books,
distributed by Outlet Book Company, Inc.,
a Random House Company, 225 Park Avenue South,
New York, New York 10003.

Printed and bound in Hong Kong

ISBN 0-517-07324-2
8 7 6 5 4 3 2 1

Aircraft

The wonders of travelling freely through the skies have only been with us for the past 80 years or so. In that time, aircraft have progressed from slow, uncontrollable balloons drifting on the breeze and clumsy machines hopping for a few metres at a time to the thrills of supersonic jet travel at more than twice the speed of sound. Now it is possible for people to travel between London and New York—a distance of 4800 km (3000 miles)—in the time it could take an average person to walk six miles. Aircraft have indeed made the world a smaller place!

As we rush headlong into the future, possibilities for the development of aircraft seem endless. Many of today's modern high-flying aircraft are practically spacecraft. The events of this century must surely have gone beyond our great grandparents' wildest dreams, so who knows what the future holds? This book attempts to explain some of the wonderful developments in the world of aircraft, past and present, in peacetime and in war.

Spitfire fighter aircraft

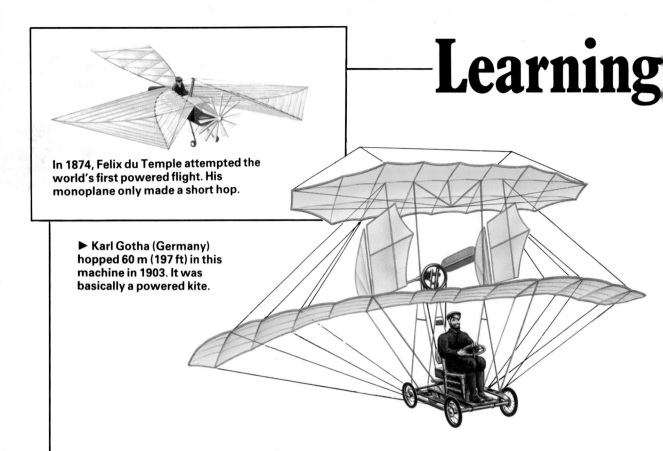

In 1874, Felix du Temple attempted the world's first powered flight. His monoplane only made a short hop.

▶ Karl Gotha (Germany) hopped 60 m (197 ft) in this machine in 1903. It was basically a powered kite.

The Birth of Flight

People have yearned to fly for thousands of years. In the distant past, our ancestors looked up into the sky and wondered how birds could fly so easily. Many tried to copy birds by strapping wings to their arms and jumping off hilltops or tall buildings. But no matter how hard they flapped their arms, they were more likely to crash to the ground than fly. This was (and is) because human muscles are just not strong enough to overcome the pull of the Earth.

None of these people understood the *principles of flight*. They did not know that birds stay up in the air because *lift* is generated as their wings move forward. And all the sculling action of their wingtip feathers does is provide *thrust* to propel them through the air.

The breakthrough came in the early 19th century. In 1804, Sir George Cayley realized that a kite's surface provides lift. He attached a kite to a long stick, added a moveable tail and finally a small balancing weight to the front. This was the first glider.

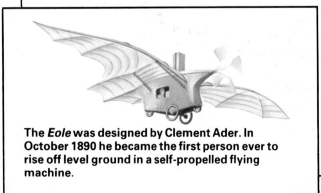

The *Eole* was designed by Clement Ader. In October 1890 he became the first person ever to rise off level ground in a self-propelled flying machine.

▶ William Henson's futuristic drawing of *Ariel*, an aerial steam carriage, was published in 1843. Later he built working models.

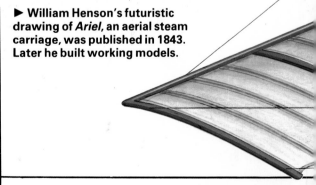

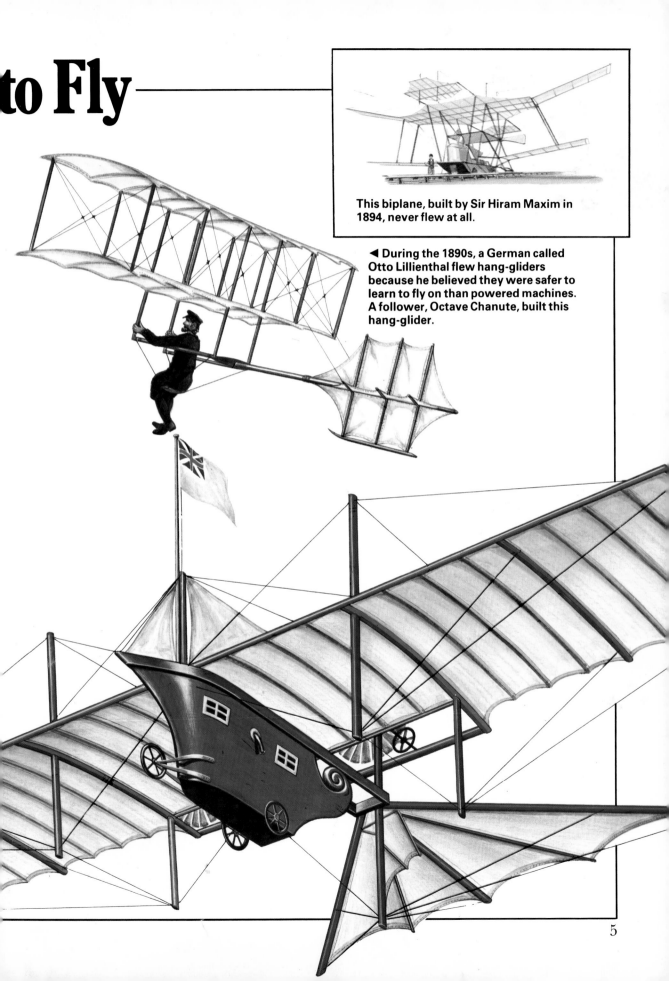

to Fly

This biplane, built by Sir Hiram Maxim in 1894, never flew at all.

◄ During the 1890s, a German called Otto Lillienthal flew hang-gliders because he believed they were safer to learn to fly on than powered machines. A follower, Octave Chanute, built this hang-glider.

The Wright Way

Orville and Wilbur Wright became interested in the problem of flight around 1896. At the time, they ran a cycle-building business in Dayton, Ohio, USA. By 1899 they had learned enough about the attempts of others to begin experiments of their own. They first built a small biplane kite (or glider) with a wingspan of just 1·5 m (5 ft). Its flights were successful because the Wrights had discovered a way to control the direction in which it flew. They warped the glider's wingtips by remote control while it was in the air.

By 1900, they had built a much bigger glider. This was shipped to the bleak sand

▲ On 14 December 1903, Wilbur Wright (1867-1912) attempted the first powered flight in the original *Flyer*. Unfortunately, it crashed after 3½ seconds in the air.

Wings covered with unbleached muslin

Twin rudders for steering

Elevator control lever

Pilot operated warp control wires by moving his body from side to side

How it Flew

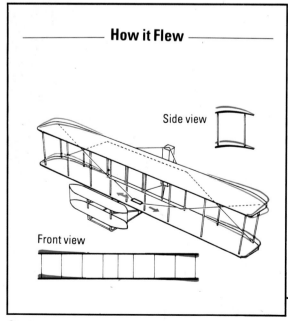

Side view

Front view

▲ The original Wright *Flyer*. This had a wingspan of 12·29 m (40 ft 4 in), a length of 6·43 m (21 ft 1 in), and a flying weight of about 338 kg (746 lb). *Flyer No. 3*, which followed in 1905, was the world's first practical aeroplane.

hills of Kitty Hawk, North Carolina. Most of the time it was flown as a kite, although a few flights were made with one of the brothers aboard. By the following year—when their second glider was built—they had realized that much of the information they were relying on was mistaken and misleading. So they built a wind-tunnel at home to research into the problems of controlling an aircraft. As a result, their next experimental glider, built in 1902, made hundreds of successful flights. Soon, work was started on the *Flyer*—the powered aircraft that would earn them a leading place in the history of aviation.

The First Flyers

Flyer No. 1, the Wright brothers' original powered flying-machine, was a larger version of their third glider. Its power came from a specially built 12 hp petrol engine which was mounted on the lower wing and drove two pusher propellers through a system of bicycle chains. Its first four successful flights were all made on Thursday, 17 December, 1903.

The more advanced *Flyer No. 2* followed in 1904. This could make turns and fly a circuit. And by this time their flights were lasting up to five minutes.

Flyer No. 3 was built in 1905. In tests it stayed airborne for up to 38 minutes and covered a distance of 39 km (24 miles). It was followed by the *Flyer No. 4*—seven of which had been built by 1908. One of these was taken to France and flown in front of a European audience by Wilbur. The Europeans—who hadn't even known that flight-control was necessary—were amazed!

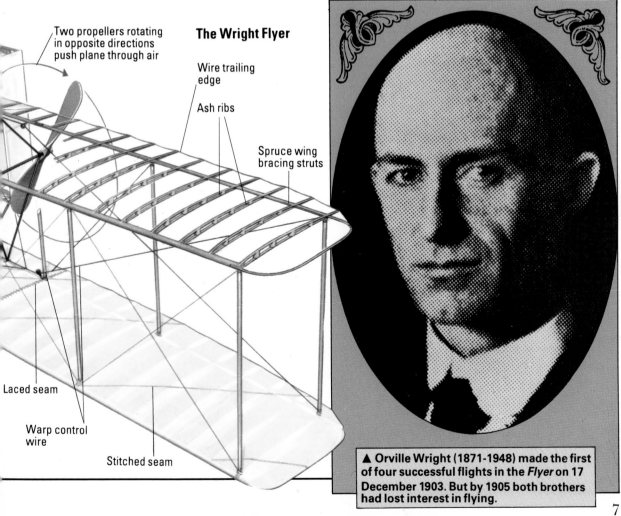

The Wright Flyer

Two propellers rotating in opposite directions push plane through air

Wire trailing edge

Ash ribs

Spruce wing bracing struts

Laced seam

Warp control wire

Stitched seam

▲ Orville Wright (1871-1948) made the first of four successful flights in the *Flyer* on 17 December 1903. But by 1905 both brothers had lost interest in flying.

7

Pioneering Planes

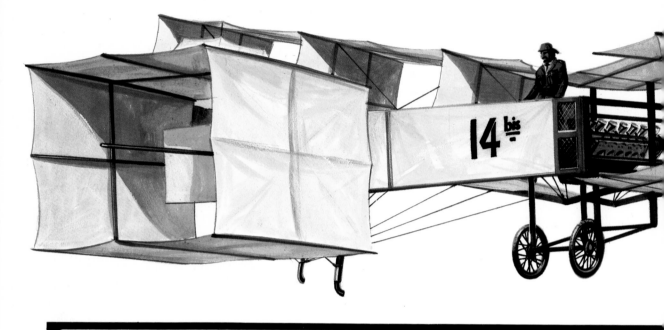

▲ The complicated *Aéroplane*, designed in 1908 by Captain Dorand for military use.

▼ In November 1908, the American Glenn Curtiss tried and failed to turn *June Bug* into a seaplane by fitting floats.

Few people took much notice of the Wright brothers' historic flight in 1903. In Europe, experimenters still refused to believe that aviators needed to know about aerodynamics or that planes needed special controls to make them work. Then in 1905, the Wright brothers retired from aviation for a short while and the focus of attention shifted from America to Europe.

In 1906 a Brazilian airship pioneer called Alberto Santos-Dumont stepped into the limelight. He had a strange-looking aircraft—the *14 bis*—built for him by Gabriel

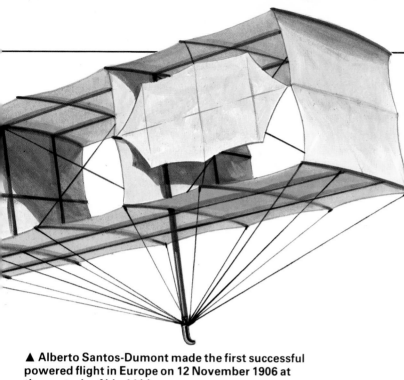

▲ Alberto Santos-Dumont made the first successful powered flight in Europe on 12 November 1906 at the controls of his *14 bis*.

Voisin. In October 1906 he flew this for a distance of 60 m (197 ft) and won a prize for being the first person in Europe to fly more than 25 m (80 ft). All at once, France became the centre of world aviation. In 1907, the Voisins unveiled a Henri Farman no. 1 design which became one of the most widely used aircraft of its time. In fact, Farman himself won 50,000 francs in the following year by flying his aircraft around a closed one kilometre (0·62 mile) circuit.

On 25 July 1909, Louis Blériot set off to cross the English Channel from Calais to Dover in his home-built monoplane, and completed the trip in about 38 minutes. This earned him world-wide publicity and a £1000 prize from the *Daily Mail* newspaper. The following month the world's first air races were held at Rheims, France. All the leading pilots of the day attended—including Louis Blériot, Henri Farman and Glenn H. Curtiss.

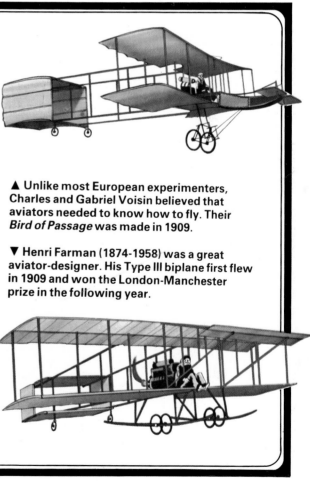

▲ Unlike most European experimenters, Charles and Gabriel Voisin believed that aviators needed to know how to fly. Their *Bird of Passage* was made in 1909.

▼ Henri Farman (1874-1958) was a great aviator-designer. His Type III biplane first flew in 1909 and won the London-Manchester prize in the following year.

World War I

◄ A British Sopwith Camel. With over 1294 'kills' these were the most successful fighters of the war.

► The 190 km/h (120 mph) Fokker D VII was Germany's best fighter of the war.

► Over 15,000 of these Spad fighters were built and flown by all the Allied air forces.

▼ This scene shows a British SE 5 being attacked in a dog-fight by one of Germany's crack Albatros fighters.

the Air

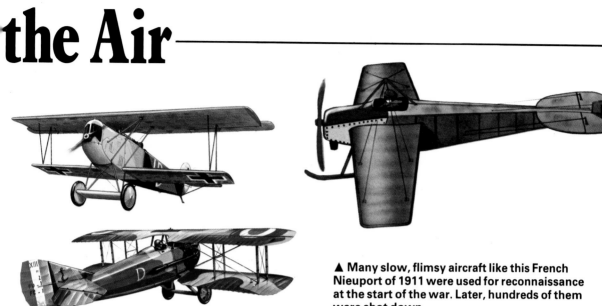

▲ Many slow, flimsy aircraft like this French Nieuport of 1911 were used for reconnaissance at the start of the war. Later, hundreds of them were shot down.

When World War 1 broke out in 1914, aircraft were such new inventions that most people had never even seen one. The world's air forces had only around 850 machines between them—and none of these was designed to carry any weapons. But heavier-than-air craft soon showed their worth as scouts over enemy lines. From their open cockpits, crews could photograph the battlefields and use signals or radios to direct the aim of their artillery down below. Then, inevitably, some flyers began to shoot at each other with hand-held guns. Others took to dropping bricks, steel darts, grenades or high-explosive shells by hand on their enemy's positions. And so the idea of 'air power' was born, and with it the first-ever warplanes designed and built as specialized fighters or bombers. By the end of the war, in 1918, tens of thousands of aircraft had taken part. Many could fly at over 200 km/h (120 mph), while some fighters were armed with six heavy machine-guns. There were also bombers that could fly halfway across Europe with loads of several thousand kilogrammes. Rapid development indeed — in just four years.

The Aces

Although their machines sometimes flew at up to 240 km/h (150 mph) about 6150 m (20,000 ft) over the Earth, hardly any World War 1 aircrew ever carried parachutes. They could be killed just as easily by an engine breakdown as by an enemy bullet in the fuel tanks. In fact, the life-expectancy of pilots was often down to just two weeks. Whole formations of planes sometimes met, and in the dog-fights that followed, dozens might plunge down in pieces or in flames. So, among the ranks of the short-lived fighter pilots, anyone who shot down five or more enemy aircraft was called an 'ace' and treated as a hero. Aces were sometimes 'natural' flyers or crack marksmen, but often they were simply flying a new type of aircraft which was better than its opposition. When the enemy in turn brought out a better type, new aces usually emerged as the old ones were killed off.

These pilots were some of the best-known aces:
- **Germany:** Manfred von Richthofen, the 'Red Baron' (80 kills); Ernst Udet (62 kills); Oswald Boelcke (40 kills); Max Immelman (15 kills).
- **Britain:** Mick Mannock (73 kills); Billy Bishop (72 kills); Albert Ball (44 kills).
- **France:** Réné Fonck (75 kills); Georges Guynemer (54 kills); Charles Nungesser (45 kills).
- **Russia:** Captain Kazakov (17 kills).
- **USA:** Eddie Rickenbacker (26 kills).

Amazing Flights

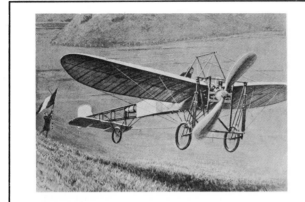

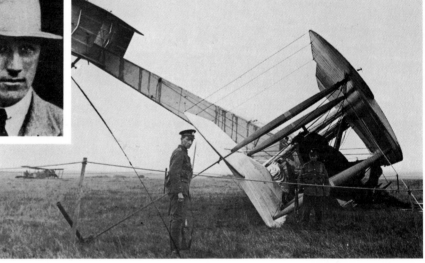

◀ When, on 25 July 1909, Blériot took off from Calais to cross the English Channel, no one knew whether or not he would reach Dover, 38 km (23·5 miles) away. Apart from still suffering pain from injuries received in an earlier crash, he had no real navigational aids to help him find his way through the thick sea mists. When he reached Dover 37 minutes later, his plane crash-landed on to the clifftops near Dover Castle. The following year saw the first non-stop double crossing of the Channel. This time the pilot was C.S. Rolls (the Rolls of Rolls Royce).

▲ On 14 June 1919, John Alcock and Arthur Whitten Brown took off from Newfoundland in a modified Vickers Vimy Bomber. Their non-stop flight across the Atlantic to Clifden, Ireland, took 16 hours 27½ minutes.

▼ The *Spirit of St Louis*, which carried Lindbergh on his solo non-stop Atlantic flight, now hangs in the National Air and Space Museum in Washington, DC, USA.

◀ Charles Lindbergh, the first man to fly solo across the Atlantic (1927).

The Shrinking World

- **1911**: The first non-stop flight from London to Paris was made on 12 April 1911. Pierre Prier took less than four hours to cover the 402 km (251 miles) in his Blériot monoplane.

  Calbraith P. Rodgers became the first man to fly coast-to-coast over America. His Wright biplane carried him 6437 km (4000 miles) in 82 flying hours over 49 days. His plane crashed 19 times during the journey, but luckily he was followed by a special train containing spares.

  Harriet Quimby, an American, was the first woman to fly solo across the Channel.

  Frank McClean flew a Short floatplane under Tower Bridge, London. When he landed on the River Thames by Westminster, he was questioned by the police (like everyone else who has performed this stunt since then).

- **1913**: Roland Garros became the first man to cross the Mediterranean by air. He flew from Southern France to Tunisia—a distance of 729 km (435 miles)—in less than eight hours.

- **1914**: Tryggve Gran, a Norwegian pilot, was the first man to fly over the North Sea. He flew in a Blériot.

  Most civil flying stopped in Europe until after World War 1. However, South America was not involved in this 'war to end all wars'.

- **1918**: Teniente Candelana, an Argentinian Army pilot made the first aerial crossing of the Andes from east to west on 13 April. He reached an altitude of 3960 m (13,600 ft) in his Morane aircraft.

  On 12 December, a Chilean pilot called Teniente Godoy crossed the Andes from west to east in a Bristol monoplane.

▲ Handley Page HP 42. In 1931, Imperial Airways began using this early, purpose-built airliner on its European and Egypt–India and Egypt–Central Africa routes.

▲ In 1930, Amy Johnson flew her 100 horsepower de Havilland Moth *Jason* from Britain to Australia. She was the first woman to fly halfway across this planet by herself.

▲ The first flight over the Pacific was made in 1928 by two Australians, Charles Kingsford Smith and Charles Ulm. Their aeroplane was a Fokker monoplane, *Southern Cross*.

13

Battle for the Skies

Warplanes played quite a small part in World War 1, and they did not affect its outcome. However, in World War 2 (1939-45) they were one of the major weapons. By then, fast, heavily-armed fighters had been developed that could often carry bombs or rockets as well. Bombers, too, had become fast and high-flying, and could haul tonnes of explosives thousands of kilometres. A wide range of other specialized weapons had also emerged. These included photo-reconnaissance fighters, ground-attackers and 'tank-busters' armed with artillery guns; torpedo-bombers and dive-bombers which screamed down from the sun to destroy their targets. All the warring countries raced against each other to build better warplanes, and so the war years saw fantastic 'improvements' in all-round performance. Radar, electronic systems, carrier warfare, jet power and pressurization were some of the other important features of air warfare developed at this time.

Famous air actions of the war included the Battle of Britain, Pearl Harbor, the German *blitz* of Britain, the British and American 'area bombing' of German cities and the Battle of Midway between the Pacific carrier fleets of Japan and the USA. And in 1945, America's B-29 Superfortress bombers, with their ranges of well over 5000 km (3000 miles) dropped the world's first atomic bombs on the Japanese cities of Hiroshima and Nagasaki. Amid terrible destruction, World War 2 came to an end.

P-51 Mustang

"Dallas Doll"

Messerschmitt Bf 109

Famous Fighters

Some of the main designs of World War 2 fighter aircraft (and their top speeds in km/h/mph) were the following:

Britain: Hawker Hurricane (545/349); Supermarine Spitfire (721/448); Hawker Typhoon (671/417); Gloster Meteor (793/493).

USA: Curtiss P-40 Warhawk/Kittyhawk (563/350); Lockheed P-38 Lightning (665/415); Republic P-47 Thunderbolt (690/429); North American P-51 Mustang (703/437).

Germany: Messerschmitt Bf 109 (689/428); Messerschmitt Bf 110 (550/342); jet-powered Me 262 (869/540); Focke-Wulf Fw 190 (656/408).

Japan: Nakajima Ki-43 (512/320) and Ki-84 (612/380); Mitsubishi A6M Zero Sen (565/351).

Russia: Yakovlev Yak-9 (578/359); Mikoyan MiG-3 (650/405); Ilyushin Il-2 Stormovik (434/270); Lavochkin La-7 (660/413).

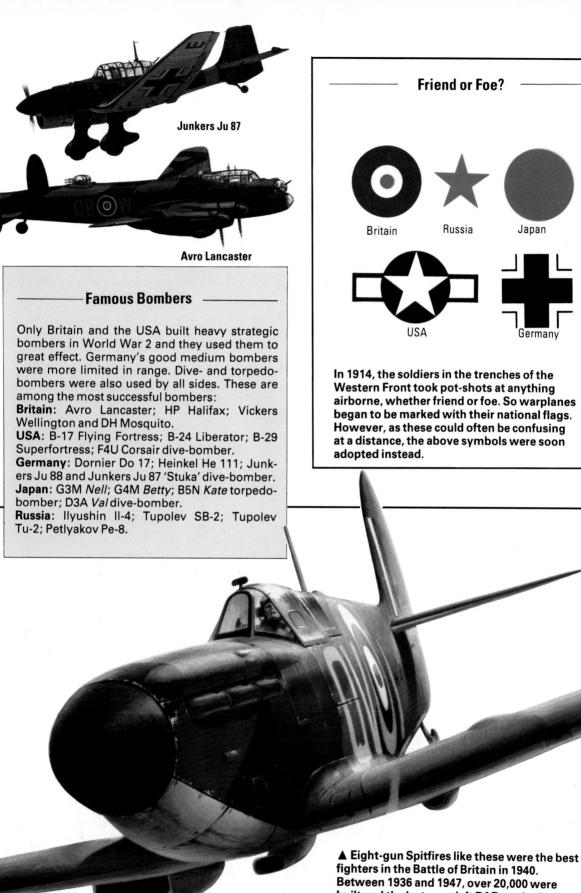

Junkers Ju 87

Avro Lancaster

Famous Bombers

Only Britain and the USA built heavy strategic bombers in World War 2 and they used them to great effect. Germany's good medium bombers were more limited in range. Dive- and torpedo-bombers were also used by all sides. These are among the most successful bombers:

Britain: Avro Lancaster; HP Halifax; Vickers Wellington and DH Mosquito.
USA: B-17 Flying Fortress; B-24 Liberator; B-29 Superfortress; F4U Corsair dive-bomber.
Germany: Dornier Do 17; Heinkel He 111; Junkers Ju 88 and Junkers Ju 87 'Stuka' dive-bomber.
Japan: G3M *Nell*; G4M *Betty*; B5N *Kate* torpedo-bomber; D3A *Val* dive-bomber.
Russia: Ilyushin Il-4; Tupolev SB-2; Tupolev Tu-2; Petlyakov Pe-8.

Friend or Foe?

Britain Russia Japan

USA Germany

In 1914, the soldiers in the trenches of the Western Front took pot-shots at anything airborne, whether friend or foe. So warplanes began to be marked with their national flags. However, as these could often be confusing at a distance, the above symbols were soon adopted instead.

▲ Eight-gun Spitfires like these were the best fighters in the Battle of Britain in 1940. Between 1936 and 1947, over 20,000 were built and the last ones left RAF service in 1954.

How to Stay in the Air

◄ The biggest airliner of all time is the 356,070 kg (785,000 lb) Boeing 747 'jumbo jet'. It can carry 500 people for more than 10,000 km (6500 miles) at speeds of around 978 km/h (608 mph). The first 747s flew in 1969.

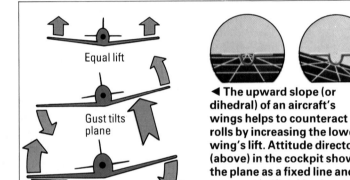

Equal lift

Gust tilts plane

Increased lift corrects tilt

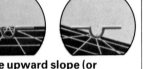

◄ The upward slope (or dihedral) of an aircraft's wings helps to counteract rolls by increasing the lower wing's lift. Attitude directors (above) in the cockpit show the plane as a fixed line and have an 'artificial horizon' which moves to stay parallel to the Earth's surface. So the angle of banking can be seen at a glance.

The Aerofoil

An aerofoil—such as an aircraft's wing or a helicopter's rotor blade—is something which creates lift when it moves through the air. It does this by making the air travel further over its curved upper surface than it does under the lower, flat surface. As a result, air pressure is higher beneath than above the aerofoil. This creates a sort of upward suction which makes the wing or rotor rise together with the aircraft. The illustration below shows a cross-section of an aerofoil and also the pattern of the airflow around it.

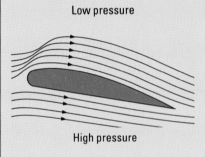

Low pressure

High pressure

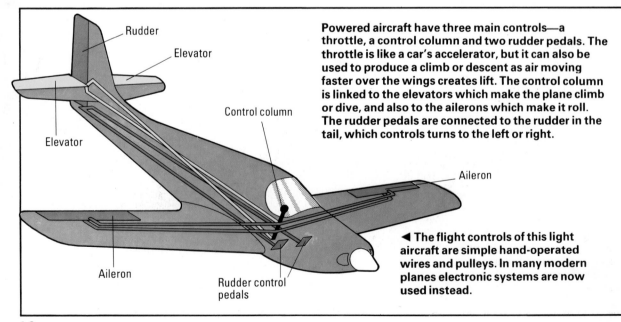

Rudder

Elevator

Control column

Elevator

Powered aircraft have three main controls—a throttle, a control column and two rudder pedals. The throttle is like a car's accelerator, but it can also be used to produce a climb or descent as air moving faster over the wings creates lift. The control column is linked to the elevators which make the plane climb or dive, and also to the ailerons which make it roll. The rudder pedals are connected to the rudder in the tail, which controls turns to the left or right.

Aileron

Aileron

Rudder control pedals

◄ The flight controls of this light aircraft are simple hand-operated wires and pulleys. In many modern planes electronic systems are now used instead.

High

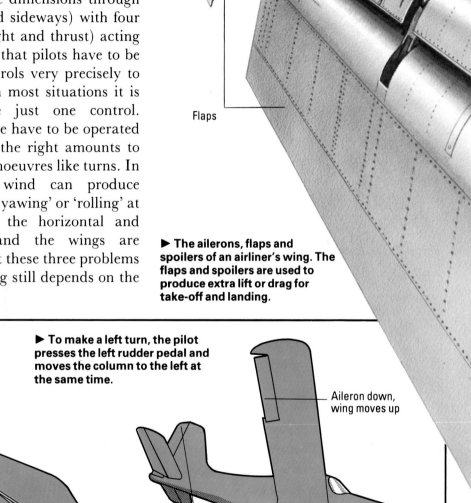

Spoilers

Ailerons

Flaps

Flying an aircraft is not as simple as driving a car. Technically speaking, this is because aircraft move in three dimensions through the air (up, down and sideways) with four forces (lift, drag, weight and thrust) acting on them. This means that pilots have to be able to use their controls very precisely to stay airborne. And in most situations it is not enough to use just one control. Normally, two or three have to be operated together and by just the right amounts to make even simple manoeuvres like turns. In addition, gusts of wind can produce dangerous 'pitching', 'yawing' or 'rolling' at any time. Although the horizontal and vertical tailplanes and the wings are designed to counteract these three problems respectively, safe flying still depends on the pilot's skill.

▶ The ailerons, flaps and spoilers of an airliner's wing. The flaps and spoilers are used to produce extra lift or drag for take-off and landing.

▶ To make a left turn, the pilot presses the left rudder pedal and moves the column to the left at the same time.

Aileron down, wing moves up

▲ Pushing the column forward moves the elevators down. The airflow over them then pushes the tail up so that the plane dives down.

Rudder left, tail moves right

Aileron up, wing moves down

17

Air and Ground Control

The Flight Director arrives at the airport 30 minutes before any other crew member. He or she checks on weather conditions so that mealtimes can be planned around bad weather. He also gets a list from terminal control of any VIPs and other special passengers on the flight. About an hour before the aircraft departs, the flight crew arrive. The Captain and First Officer go to flight dispatch to be briefed on weather conditions and on recommended and available routes. The Engineer goes to the aircraft to check the fuelling. When passengers and crew have boarded, the doors are closed and the air jetty moved.

The Captain and aircraft crew carry out routine pre-flight checks. At the same time, an airport official makes sure that all service vehicles—except the mobile generator that supplies power to start the engines—are out of the way. When the aircraft is ready to leave, the Captain radios the ground controller for permission to start the engines. Then the Captain asks ground control for clearance to move across the apron to the taxiway. The Captain is told which taxiways and runway to use.

At the end of the runway, the crew wait for take-off clearance from Air Traffic Control. Then, keeping the brakes on and engines opened up, the Captain makes more pre-flight checks. Finally, the brakes are released and the aircraft speeds along the runway. Once in the air, the aircraft passes through height bands according to air traffic control's instructions. At each, the First Officer reports the height and is given clearance for the next required altitude. If ground control wishes to get in touch with the aircraft, they do this through Selcal (Selective Calling) to the aircraft's permanent call-sign.

▶ The flight deck of a Boeing 747 jumbo jet liner. The instruments show important details like the engines' performance, the aircraft's course, position and height above the Earth, and whether it is flying straight and level. The Instrument Landing System can also land the aircraft automatically in very bad weather. On many advanced aircraft, this information is shown on a screen called a HDD (Head Down Display). Both pilot and co-pilot have a control column which operates the ailerons, elevators and a rudder bar. Between the pilots are the throttles which control the engines.

Airport roads

Control tower

go terminal

Pier

Terminal building

Apron

Taxiway

Runway

Inside an Airport

── Air Crashes ──

When an airliner crashes anywhere in the world, the story is widely reported in newspapers. As a result, many people think airliners are accident-prone and re- fuse to fly in them. In fact, this is not the case, and travelling by air is actually much safer than crossing the road. Statistics show us that an airline pilot would have to live to be about 400 years old before seriously expecting to be in an accident. Put another way, in 1975 the world's airlines flew about 7550 million km (4691 million miles) and there were just 21 crashes which killed 473 passengers. Nevertheless, few people survive an airlin- er crash.

In the early days of jet travel, the prob- lems of metal fatigue were not understood, and as a result three Comet 1s broke up in mid-air in 1953-54. In the late 1970s wide- bodied DC-10s started to lose parts, such as engines, in flight. However, as technolo- gy improves, the greatest single danger remains 'human error' such as that which, in 1979, caused a DC-10 with almost 400 people on board, to crash off-course into an Antarctic mountain.

▲ When an aircraft is on final approach and lined up with its landing runway, it is transferred from approach control to the airport control tower who bring it in to land. The tower controller uses a radar display which is measured in nautical miles. As the aircraft approaches to land, its movements are shown by a blip on the screen. During the night, runway lights guide pilots in to land.

Jet Power

The earliest forerunner of today's gas-turbine aero-engines was a design made by an Englishman, John Barberin, in 1791. This used spinning fans to produce a jet of hot gases. In those days though, the heat and strains of this engine would have been too much for the available metals or engineering skills. As a result, it was never built. During 1917 the first small experimental gas-turbine engines were built by scientists in Britain. By the 1930s, military planners had realized that there were limits to the speed and height at which the earlier piston-engined warplanes could fly. With war approaching, research was urgently increased.

Finally, in 1937, a young RAF officer called Frank Whittle built the world's first working gas-turbine aero-engine. This was used in an experimental aircraft (the E.28/39) in 1941, and an improved version was used to power the twin-engined Gloster Meteor fighter. This fought successfully in the last year of World War 2. By then, though, it had been joined by a number of German jet warplanes. These included the Messerschmitt Me 262 and Me163, the Arado Ar 234 and the Heinkel He 162.

The Americans in turn copied Whittle's designs and built the Bell P-59 Airacomet, but this was perfected too late to see war service.

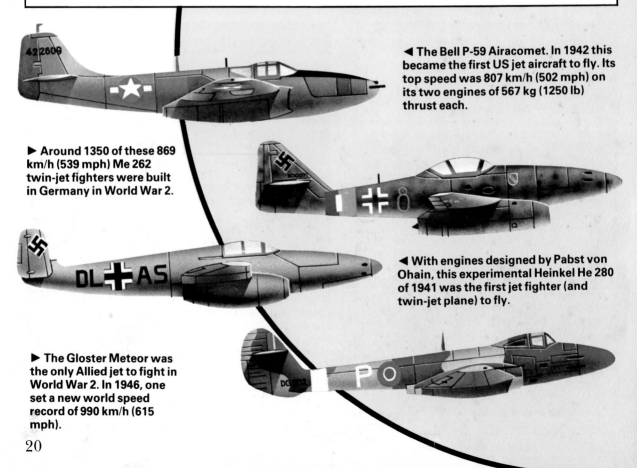

◄ The Bell P-59 Airacomet. In 1942 this became the first US jet aircraft to fly. Its top speed was 807 km/h (502 mph) on its two engines of 567 kg (1250 lb) thrust each.

► Around 1350 of these 869 km/h (539 mph) Me 262 twin-jet fighters were built in Germany in World War 2.

◄ With engines designed by Pabst von Ohain, this experimental Heinkel He 280 of 1941 was the first jet fighter (and twin-jet plane) to fly.

► The Gloster Meteor was the only Allied jet to fight in World War 2. In 1946, one set a new world speed record of 990 km/h (615 mph).

Jet Flight

The simplest sort of jet engines are ramjets. They have no fans or turbines and air is just squeezed into the tube as it moves through the air. V-1 'doodlebugs' used ramjets.

Turbojets are noisier and less powerful than turbofans but they were long preferred for warplanes because they are smaller and easy to fit with afterburners.

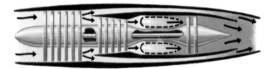

Bypass (or turbofan) jet engines have huge fans at the front to suck in vast amounts of air. Some of this bypasses the combustion chamber and then re-joins the exhaust gases. The result is much greater thrust.

Turboprop engines produce jet thrust like turbojets, but their turbines also drive a propeller. They are more economical but slower than pure jets, and were popular for transport aircraft.

▼ The Rolls Royce RB-211 turbofan produces 20,411 kg (45,000 lb) of thrust. TriStars use three turbofans.

Aircraft jet engines suck air in at one end of a tube and force it out of the other end at a much greater speed. As a result, the engine—and with it the plane—is thrust in the opposite direction. To speed up the air passing through the tube, jet engines have powerful fans (or turbines) inside to compress the air. The air is then mixed with fuel and exploded by a spark. The heat of the explosion makes the air expand suddenly and, to escape from the enclosed tube, it rushes out of the back of the tube. The force of this red-hot exhaust creates an amount of forward thrust measured in kilogrammes, not horsepower.

Nowadays there are two main types of gas-turbine aero-engines—turbojets and turbofans. Many also have afterburners which add more fuel to the escaping gases as they leave the back of the engine and re-explode them to increase the thrust.

Breaking the Sound Barrier

Jet Age

◀ After a terrific battering, this American rocket-powered Bell X-1 (piloted by Charles Yeager) became the first aircraft to 'break the sound barrier' in 1947.

In the years following World War 2, countries like the USA, Russia and Britain raced to increase the power of their jet engines. With top speeds of around 844 km/h (525 mph), fighters of the 1940s such as Britain's Vampire, America's F-80 Shooting Star and Russia's Yak-15 were among the first results of this competition. Next came the leap to 600 mph (965 km/h) — with machines such as the American F-86 Sabre, Russia's MiG-15, Sweden's Saab J29 and Britain's Hunter. By the early 1950s, equally fast jet bombers such as America's B-45 Tornado and B-47 Stratojet, Russia's Il-28 and Britain's Canberra and V-bombers had also appeared. Then, in 1953, both America's F-100 Super Sabre and Russia's MiG-19 went supersonic in level flight — and a new race had begun.

▼ This diagram shows how the speed of aircraft has gone up since World War 2. The speed of sound, Mach 1, is 1223 km/h (760 mph) at sea level. At higher altitudes, though, sound travels more slowly. So at 11,000 m (36,000 ft) Mach 1 is 1062 km/h (660 mph). The Mach unit is named after the Austrian scientist, Dr Ernest Mach (1838-1916), who worked it out.

▶ For supersonic flight, swept or delta wings (like Concorde's) are necessary as straight wings set up too much resistance to the air. In fact, Concorde can cruise at Mach 2·04—over twice the speed of sound at high altitude.

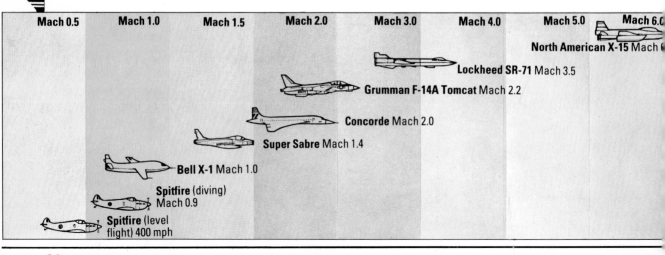

| Mach 0.5 | Mach 1.0 | Mach 1.5 | Mach 2.0 | Mach 3.0 | Mach 4.0 | Mach 5.0 | Mach 6.0 |

North American X-15 Mach 6

Lockheed SR-71 Mach 3.5

Grumman F-14A Tomcat Mach 2.2

Concorde Mach 2.0

Super Sabre Mach 1.4

Bell X-1 Mach 1.0

Spitfire (diving) Mach 0.9

Spitfire (level flight) 400 mph

▲ The British Fairey Delta 2 research aircraft shot the world absolute speed record to well over 1000 mph (1609 km/h) in 1956.

▲ Russia was slow to build big jets in the 1950s, but it did produce the 877 km/h (545 mph) Tu-114—the world's fastest propeller-driven aircraft.

Jet Speed Records

		km/h	mph
1946	Gloster Meteor F4	990·79	615·65
1947	Lockheed F-80	1003·60	623·61
	Douglas Skystreak	1047·33	650·78
1948	North American F-86 Sabre	1079·61	670·84
1953	North American F-86 Sabre	1151·64	715·60
	Hawker Hunter 3	1170·76	727·48
	Supermarine Swift 4	1183·74	735·54
	North American F-100 Super Sabre	1215·04	755·00
1955	North American F-100 Super Sabre	1323·03	822·10
1956	Fairey Delta 2	1821·39	1132·00
1957	McDonnell F-101 Voodoo	1943·03	1207·34
1958	Lockheed F-104 Starfighter	2259·18	1403·80
1959	Mikoyan E-66	2387·48	1483·51
	Convair F-106 Delta Dart	2455·74	1525·93
1961	McDonnell F-4 Phantom II	2585·43	1606·51
1962	Mikoyan E-166	2681·00	1665·90
1965	Lockheed YF-12A (Blackbird)	3331·51	2070·10

Passenger Aircraft

Only the rich were able to afford air travel until the appearance of big jets like Boeing's 707 in the late 1950s. In the interwar years the planes may have been slow, but their passengers (see right) certainly travelled in style—often with *cordon bleu* chefs and sleeping berths. Nowadays, mass air travel has brought with it the cramped comfort of economy-class cabins such as these, inside a Lockheed TriStar.

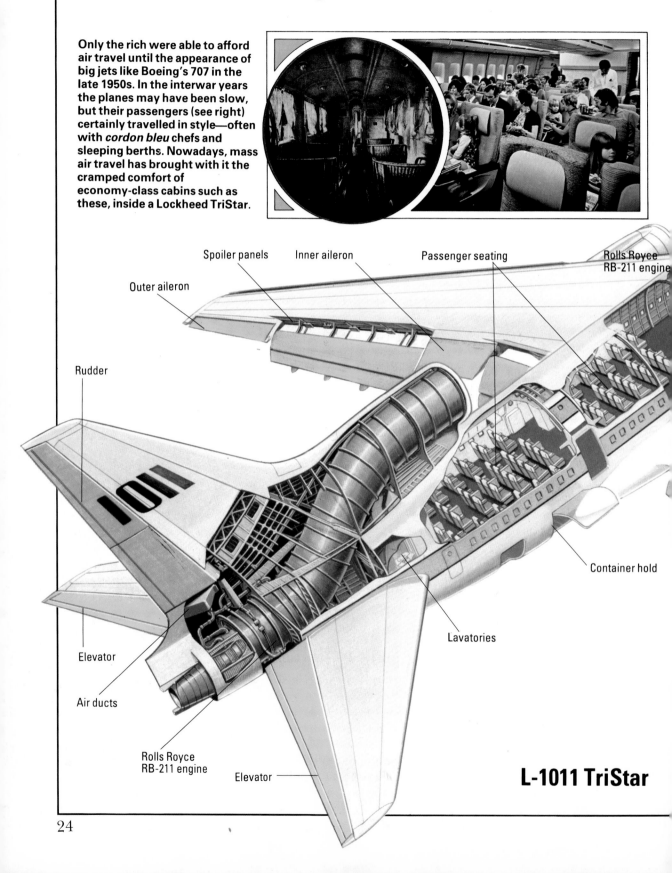

Spoiler panels

Inner aileron

Passenger seating

Rolls Royce RB-211 engine

Outer aileron

Rudder

Container hold

Elevator

Lavatories

Air ducts

Rolls Royce RB-211 engine

Elevator

L-1011 TriStar

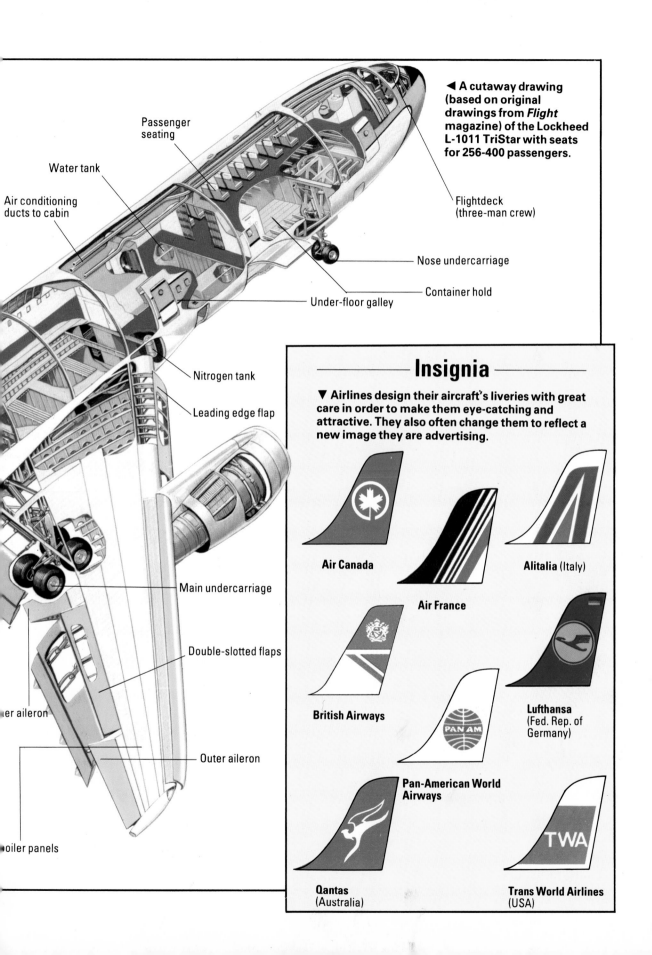

Passenger seating

Water tank

Air conditioning ducts to cabin

◀ A cutaway drawing (based on original drawings from *Flight* magazine) of the Lockheed L-1011 TriStar with seats for 256-400 passengers.

Flightdeck (three-man crew)

Nose undercarriage

Container hold

Under-floor galley

Nitrogen tank

Leading edge flap

Main undercarriage

Double-slotted flaps

er aileron

Outer aileron

oiler panels

Insignia

▼ Airlines design their aircraft's liveries with great care in order to make them eye-catching and attractive. They also often change them to reflect a new image they are advertising.

Air Canada

Air France

Alitalia (Italy)

British Airways

Pan-American World Airways

Lufthansa (Fed. Rep. of Germany)

Qantas (Australia)

Trans World Airlines (USA)

Jumbos and Airbuses

The prices of airline tickets dropped in the late 1950s and early 1960s when big, fast, long-range jet airliners such as Boeing 707s and Douglas DC-8s appeared. As a result, the annual number of airline passengers around the world doubled from 170 to 350 million between 1960 and 1970 and it has gone on rising rapidly ever since. To cope with this demand for seats, the airlines at first simply operated more aircraft. However, before long, the airspace around major airports became dangerously overcrowded.

The Big Four

Boeing 747: In service 1970; range 10,424 km (6477 miles); speed 978 km/h (608 mph); seats for up to 550.

Douglas DC-10: In service 1971; range 5760 km (3580 miles); speed 964 km/h (599 mph); seats for 270-400.

Lockheed L-1011 TriStar: In service 1972; range 5760 km (3580 miles); speed 946 km/h (599 mph); seats for 256-400.

Airbus Industrie A300: In service 1974; range 4261 km (2648 miles); speed 668 km/h (415 mph); seats for 220-336.

▲ The Lockheed C-5 Galaxy, built in 1968, is the world's largest aeroplane. It is 75.5 m (248 ft) long and has a span of 67.8 m (223 ft).

To solve this problem, plane-makers in the mid-1960s constructed bigger, three-engined aircraft (such as Tridents and Boeing 727s) to replace many of their twin-engined types on short- or medium-distance routes. Then in 1970, the first of Boeing's 500-seat 747 'jumbo jets' began to take over from smaller airliners on the world's long-distance routes. More recently, big new turbofan engines have led to the development of giant wide-bodied 'airbuses' such as the three-jet DC-10 and TriStar, and Europe's twin-jet Airbus A300. These aircraft promise to transform short- and medium-distance air transport.

▲ Seven of these 400 km/h (250 mph) Spacelines Guppies were built from retired Boeing Stratocruiser airliners between 1962 and 1970. Originally they carried sections of US space rockets in their holds. Now only two remain.

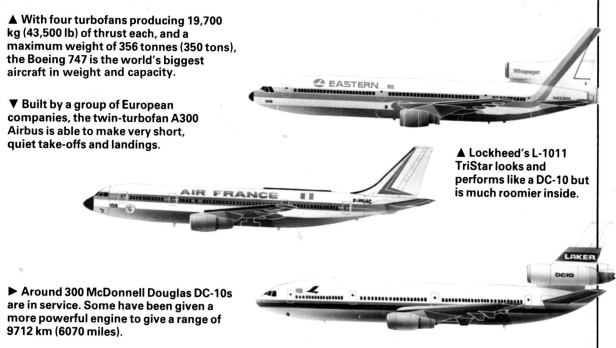

▲ With four turbofans producing 19,700 kg (43,500 lb) of thrust each, and a maximum weight of 356 tonnes (350 tons), the Boeing 747 is the world's biggest aircraft in weight and capacity.

▼ Built by a group of European companies, the twin-turbofan A300 Airbus is able to make very short, quiet take-offs and landings.

▲ Lockheed's L-1011 TriStar looks and performs like a DC-10 but is much roomier inside.

▶ Around 300 McDonnell Douglas DC-10s are in service. Some have been given a more powerful engine to give a range of 9712 km (6070 miles).

Swing-Wing

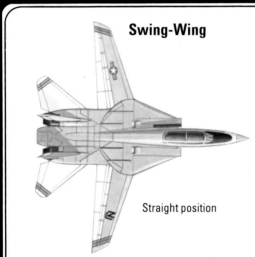

Straight position

Delta position

Delta wings are ideal for supersonic flight as they minimize drag; whereas straight wings have high drag but provide a lot of lift to make slow-speed manoeuvering, landing and take-off easier. So, to ensure that supersonic aircraft have the best wing-plan at all times the logical solution is to design them with wings that move automatically between straight and delta positions as required. The first 'swing-wing' warplane was the USAF's F-111 strike fighter of 1964. It has since been followed by Russia's MiG-23 and Su-20, the USA's F-14 Tomcat (shown above) and B-1 bomber, Europe's Tornado MRCA and others.

Vertical Take-off

Nozzles point backwards for normal flight

Britain's Hawker Siddeley Harrier is the world's only fully operational Vertical and Short Take Off and Landing (VTOL and STOL) warplane. It works by having its jet exhaust directed through four moveable nozzles which the pilot can adjust from the cockpit to point backwards (for normal forward flight), vertically down (for VTOL) or at an angle in between (for STOL).

Nozzles point downwards on take-off and landing

Modern Warplanes

Nowadays, air power is of supreme military importance, and there are many modern warplanes capable of delivering total death to the world in the form of atomic and neutron bombs. Modern air forces also include large transport aircraft which can deliver entire army divisions of invading troops and their equipment quickly to any area where there is war. And supersonic, multi-role combat planes are so well equipped with computers and integrated circuits that they can practically fly themselves. Search planes, like the USAF's Blackbird SR-71 reconnaissance aircraft, zoom around the Earth at three times the speed of sound, at a height of 19 km (12 miles). Their spy cameras can focus on an object the size of a golf-ball, anywhere on the Earth's surface. In fact, the Blackbird's cameras, radars and infra-red sensors can map 155,000 sq km (60,000 sq miles) of the Earth's surface in an hour. The Russians, who have similar aircraft, often say that if they can see a target they can hit it, and if they can hit it they can destroy it ... usually at the first attempt.

The two most modern bombers in the world today are the USSR's Tupolev Back-fire and the USA's Rockwell B-1, production of which has stopped for the moment. Their wings can swing to whatever position is needed for a particular stage of the flight.

Modern attack planes, such as the Anglo-French Jaguar and the USSR's MiG-23 can fly very low over hedges at the speed of sound, firing 6000 rounds per minute from their cannons. There are also many other types of warplane, and they all share the capability to kill or destroy their targets cleanly and efficiently.

▼ The Strikemaster light-attack aircraft was developed from the RAF's Jet Provost trainer. It carries bombs, rockets and guns (shown here) up to 700 kg (1500 lb) in weight underwing, and can fly loaded at up to 640 km/h (400 mph).

Acrobats of the Air

After World War 1, many unemployed pilots and mechanics, who had discovered the thrills and excitement of flying, searched fruitlessly for jobs connected with aviation. However, jobs then were practically non-existent because there were hardly any passenger and cargo services. Nonetheless, there were thousands of cheap war-surplus aircraft for sale. Many pilots bought their own planes and became self-employed 'barnstormers'. They travelled from place to place, often in troupes called 'Flying Circuses', and performed daring stunts in the air. From this, developed most of the basic aerobatic manoeuvres seen today at flying displays all over the world.

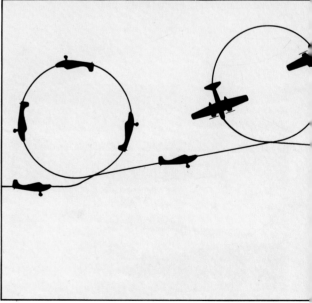

▼ The Royal Air Force's *Red Arrows* regularly perform at British and foreign meetings in their Hawker Siddeley Gnats.

Famous Stuntmen

Some airmen became famous for their own unique stunts. In 1911 the American barnstormer, Lincoln Beachey, set a new altitude record of 3529 m (11,578 ft) by climbing until he ran out of fuel and then gliding down. Geoffrey Tyson used to pick handkerchiefs off the ground with a hook suspended from his wingtip. He could fly upside down; when celebrating the 25th anniversary of Blériot's Channel crossing, he flew the whole route upside down! Charles Lindbergh would stand on the wing while his pilot flew the plane in loops. He was, of course, safely attached by invisible wires which were tied around his waist.

▲ The French Air Force's aerobatic display team, the *Patrouille de France*. This team consists of nine Magister aeroplanes which perform at meetings and air displays in France and many other European countries.

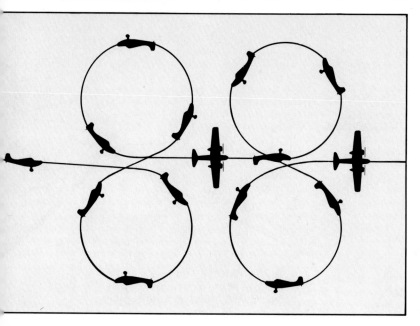

◄ This diagram shows three of the basic aerobatic manoeuvres that are performed in flying displays. From left to right these are: the Loop, which was first performed in 1913; the Cartwheel, which was first performed in 1945 and is only possible in a twin-engined plane (when the pilot reaches the top of the vertical climb, he throttles one engine back—and the plane cartwheels), and the Double Eight.

Fly to the Future

At the start of this century, the idea of people flying around the sky in machines must have seemed like a dream to almost everyone. Yet nowadays we take Concorde and jumbo jets for granted. So, to judge from history, the future of flying must be difficult to predict. It is exciting to speculate on the possibility that one day even our best jet engines will be outdated altogether by a new type of nuclear, magnetic, sonic or other source of power. In the same way, piston engines were outclassed very quickly by the development of jets. In reality, meanwhile, the era of the Space Shuttle has already dawned, and so it may not be long before space stations follow. Perhaps then—with the prospect of inter-planetary travel to lure them—people will lose interest in the business of building aircraft as we now know them.

▲ This scientist's fantasy is an 8000 km/h (5000 mph) airliner which derives most of its thrust from fuel burning on its outer skin.

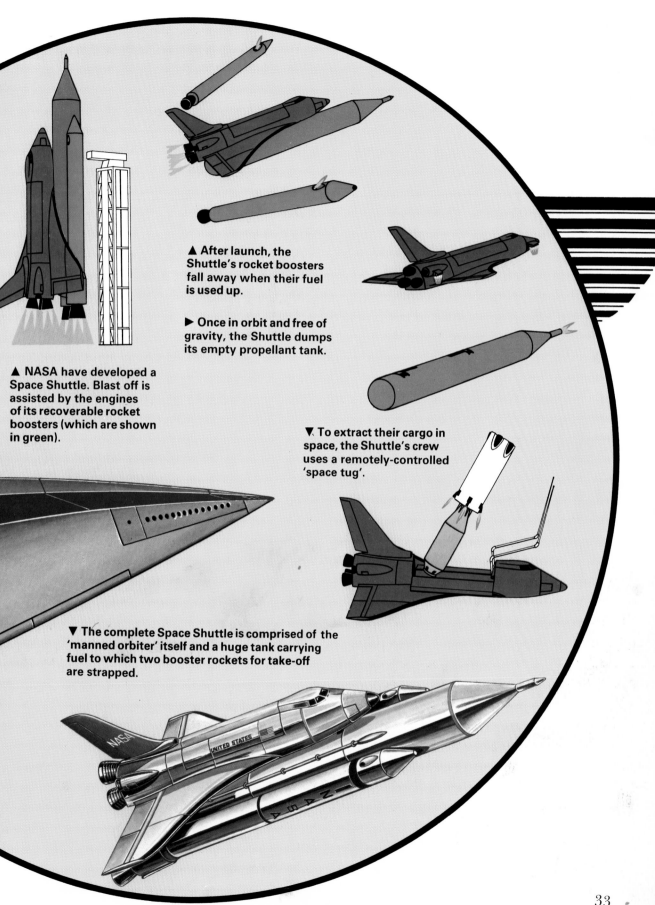

▲ After launch, the Shuttle's rocket boosters fall away when their fuel is used up.

▶ Once in orbit and free of gravity, the Shuttle dumps its empty propellant tank.

▲ NASA have developed a Space Shuttle. Blast off is assisted by the engines of its recoverable rocket boosters (which are shown in green).

▼ To extract their cargo in space, the Shuttle's crew uses a remotely-controlled 'space tug'.

▼ The complete Space Shuttle is comprised of the 'manned orbiter' itself and a huge tank carrying fuel to which two booster rockets for take-off are strapped.

Alternative

◀ On completion in March 1936, the German *Hindenburg* was the world's largest rigid airship (or dirigible). It held 75 passengers and a crew of 25. On 6 May 1937 it burst into flames while moored to a mast at Lakehurst, New Jersey, USA, after a transatlantic flight, and 36 people lost their lives.

Upper rudder

Elevator

Balloons and Airships

Lower rudder

The first lighter-than-air craft, balloons, began carrying passengers in the late 18th century. However, their major disadvantage was—and is—that they drift with the wind. Sails, oars, and even hand-driven paddles were used to try and steer them but without much success. In 1852, Henri Giffard attached a small steam engine to a spindle-shaped hydrogen-filled balloon. This was the first true non-rigid airship.

Then, in 1897, David Schwarz designed a rigid airship with an aluminium-sheet envelope. Two years later, the famous German airship designer and builder Count Ferdinand von Zeppelin began work on his first rigid airship. He was closely followed by other airship pioneers in France, America and Britain. At that time both non-rigid and rigid airships were mainly built for military use, but after World War 1 they became popular as luxury long-distance airliners. Many flew across oceans and continents, until a series of disasters in the 1930s made them very unpopular.

Wire mesh between gas bags and outer envelope

Auxiliary control room

Wooden propeller

LZ-129 Hindenburg

Aircraft

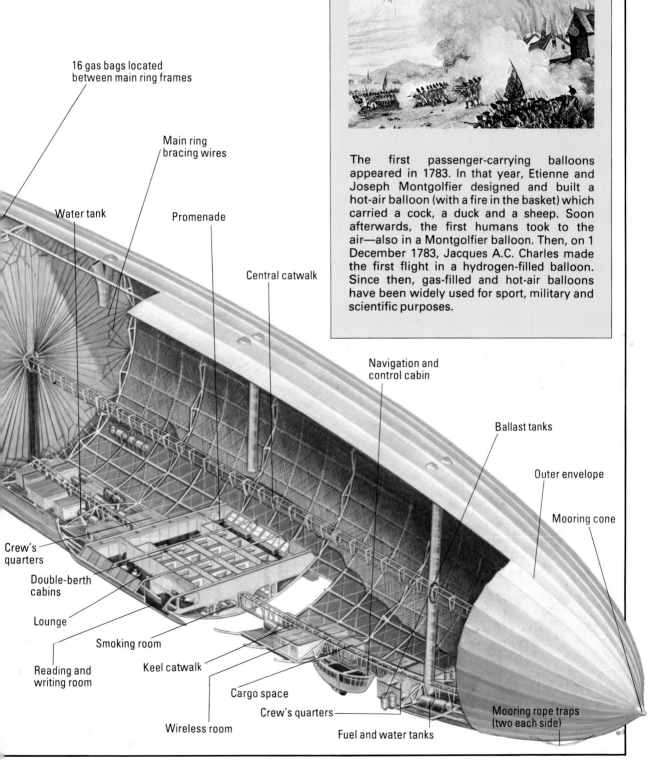

The first passenger-carrying balloons appeared in 1783. In that year, Etienne and Joseph Montgolfier designed and built a hot-air balloon (with a fire in the basket) which carried a cock, a duck and a sheep. Soon afterwards, the first humans took to the air—also in a Montgolfier balloon. Then, on 1 December 1783, Jacques A.C. Charles made the first flight in a hydrogen-filled balloon. Since then, gas-filled and hot-air balloons have been widely used for sport, military and scientific purposes.

16 gas bags located between main ring frames

Main ring bracing wires

Water tank

Promenade

Central catwalk

Navigation and control cabin

Ballast tanks

Outer envelope

Mooring cone

Crew's quarters

Double-berth cabins

Lounge

Smoking room

Keel catwalk

Reading and writing room

Cargo space

Crew's quarters

Wireless room

Fuel and water tanks

Mooring rope traps (two each side)

Helicopters and Gliders

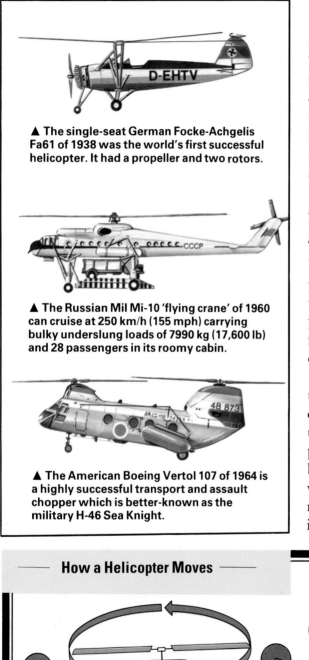

▲ The single-seat German Focke-Achgelis Fa61 of 1938 was the world's first successful helicopter. It had a propeller and two rotors.

▲ The Russian Mil Mi-10 'flying crane' of 1960 can cruise at 250 km/h (155 mph) carrying bulky underslung loads of 7990 kg (17,600 lb) and 28 passengers in its roomy cabin.

▲ The American Boeing Vertol 107 of 1964 is a highly successful transport and assault chopper which is better-known as the military H-46 Sea Knight.

Helicopters get both lift and thrust from their spinning wings, called rotors, which are driven by piston engines or jet turbines. The first design to work was the clumsy German Fa61 of 1938 (see left), but this was overshadowed by the VS-300 which first flew in 1939. Built in America by Igor Sikorski, the VS-300 set the style for most modern helicopters with its single rotor and a side-mounted propeller in the tail.

Nowadays, because they are the only aircraft that can hover at any height, helicopters have many specialized uses. They have saved countless people from burning buildings, sinking ships and other potential disasters. Many companies also use them to take bulky loads to inaccessible places, and airlines operate services to remote areas or between airports and city centres.

In addition, 'choppers' have been widely used by the military since the Korean War of 1950-53. In Vietnam, thousands were used to transport men and guns. They were particularly well suited to ferry troops into battle or recover shot-down planes and wounded or cut-off soldiers. Ship-based naval helicopters have, meanwhile, become important hunter-killers of submarines.

How a Helicopter Moves

▲ To fly upwards all the rotor blades are kept at the same angle, or pitch.

▲ To fly forward the rotor tilts forward and the blades bite the air towards the tail.

▲ Once they have been towed or winched into the air, modern gliders like this can soar for hours on the rising thermals of air.

Gliders

Soaring silently through the air with no engines of their own, gliders have to keep moving to stay aloft. If they stopped moving and stalled they would fall. So, in their design attention is paid to keeping down weight (by using materials like fibreglass or plywood), and streamlining to reduce drag. The wings must be long enough to generate plenty of lift—even at low speeds or in nearly still air. In these respects, gliders resemble birds like albatrosses and eagles which fly for hours with barely a thrust-producing flap of their long wings.

To take off, gliders either hitch a lift from a towing aircraft or are pulled along by cars or winches. Once airborne, they descend at a very gentle angle with the help of their lightweight high-lift, low-drag design. However, in the air there are often rising currents produced when winds are deflected up off hills or ridges. Warm air also rises due to convection, and such currents—called thermals—can be a great help to a glider pilot. Much of the skill of gliding lies in finding rising currents, although beginners often find landing the hardest part.

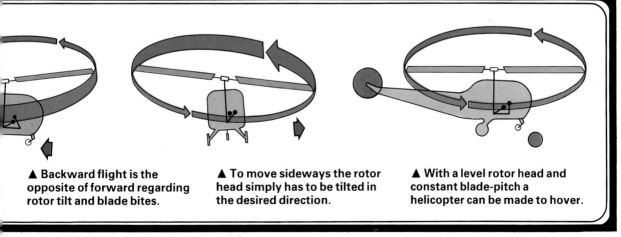

▲ Backward flight is the opposite of forward regarding rotor tilt and blade bites.

▲ To move sideways the rotor head simply has to be tilted in the desired direction.

▲ With a level rotor head and constant blade-pitch a helicopter can be made to hover.

Strange Aircraft

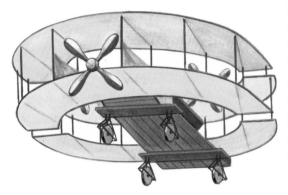

▲ This strange-looking craft, *Safety*, resembles a flying bedstead with circular biplane wings and three propellers. It was built in 1909 and probably never flew, but its research and development aided aviation technology.

▼ The Lockheed Rolls Royce Thrust Measuring Rig of 1954. It could move forward, backward and sideways at up to 48 km/h (30 mph).

People have experienced powered flight for about three quarters of a century. Whereas our ancestors could only dream of flying, we live with the reality of heavier-than-air powered aircraft. Before this time, there were no aircraft and experimenters did not have the faintest idea what an aircraft would, or should, look like. They tried every shape and form to find a workable design.

However, it was not until William Samuel Henson's impressions of an Aerial Steam Carriage were published in 1843 that people began to think of the sort of machine we know today. Even then, the designers of the earliest powered craft did not stick strictly to Henson's ideas. The *Eole*, for example, was designed and tested by Clement Ader in 1890. It had an outstanding engine and probably would have worked if the rest of the design had not been wrong. Although it had huge, bat-like wings and a semi-enclosed cabin, its only control was a steam-throttle valve!

The photographs and illustrations on these two pages show some very unusual experiments. Some are quite recent and not all of them have been disasters by any means. The Short-Mayo composite, for example, was one way of carrying enough fuel for a long-distance flight.

◄ Major Robert Mayo devised this Mayo Composite —a large Short S.21 Flying Boat *(Maia)* carrying a small four-engined Short S.20 Seaplane *(Mercury)*. Once in flight, *Mercury* was released carrying more fuel than would be possible with a conventional take-off.

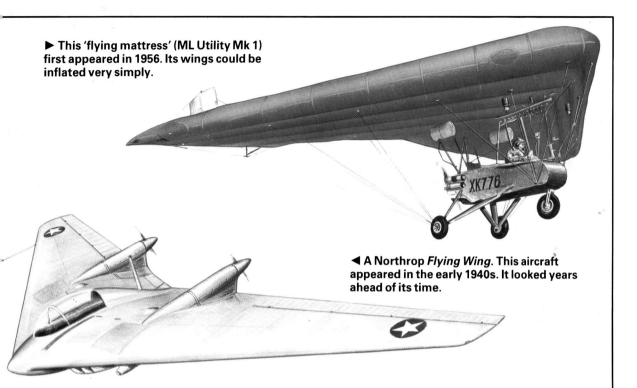

▶ This 'flying mattress' (ML Utility Mk 1) first appeared in 1956. Its wings could be inflated very simply.

◀ A Northrop *Flying Wing*. This aircraft appeared in the early 1940s. It looked years ahead of its time.

▶ Bell Aerosystems' modified Lake La-4 amphibian. When taking off or landing, this aircraft uses a cushion of air as its method of touching the ground.

▼ Designed by the Italian engineer, Caproni, this multiwing seaplane—Ca-60—could seat 100 people when it was built in 1919. However, it was too heavy to fly.

Index

Acknowledgements

Photographs: 12 Mansell Collection *top, centre left, bottom,* BBC Hulton Picture Library *centre right*; 13 BBC Hulton Picture Library 16, 18 Boeing Commercial Airplane Company; 19 Civil Aviation Authority; 21 Rolls Royce (1971) Ltd; 23 British Aircraft Corporation *bottom*, RAE Farnborough *top*; 24 Mansell Collection *top left*, British Airways *top right*; 26 RAE Farnborough *left*, Airbus Industrie *right*, 27 Japan Airlines; 28 Lockheed Aircraft Corporation; 29 Picturepoint; 30 RAE Farnborough; 34 Mansell Collection; 35 Science Museum, London; 37 Warren Jepson; 38 Rolls Royce Ltd *centre*; 39 Bell Aerospace Company.

Artwork: Michael Trim, Walter Wright, Tom Brittain, Peter Griffin, Denis Lord, Edward Hickling, John Bishop, Ron Jobson, Keith Faulkner, Graham Marks, Brian Pearce.

Picture Research: Penny Warn and Jackie Cookson.